THE QUOTABLE HOG

THE QUOTABLE HOG

By Al Clayton

LONGSTREET PRESS, INC.
Atlanta, Georgia

Published by
LONGSTREET PRESS, INC.
A subsidiary of Cox Newspapers,
A division of Cox Enterprises, Inc.
2140 Newmarket Parkway
Suite 118
Marietta, GA 30067

Printed by Arcata Graphics, Kingsport, Tennessee

1st printing 1994
Library of Congress Catalog Card Number: 93-81136
ISBN 1-56352-134-2

Cover design by Michael Taylor / Taylor Creative
Book design by Jill Dible

*F*or hog lovers everywhere, both in and out of the closet— **you** know who **you** are

INTRODUCTION

Hogs have held my attention since early childhood.

The stench rolling up from Grandma Witt's hog lot still clings to my nostrils. The slop bucket that Uncle Traynor toted down to that hog lot was no load of potpourri, either.

Now add to this the fact that years ago, a man who shot and killed my uncle right there in the mountains of Polk County, Tennessee, was "eat up by the hogs." This man shot my uncle, was sent to Brushy Mountain Penitentiary, and while working on the prison farm at the task of slopping the hogs (a form of rehabilitation), on a cold winter morning, he tripped over a log, broke his leg, and was unable to get help. The hogs ate him and the slop, too. My cousin took me to the very spot this happened, and it made a powerful impression on me. The very spot of earth seemed to be uneasy, troubled. But what could a child know?

Grandpa Clayton was crazy about hogs.

He decided to see how large a hog he could raise, and by most standards the man was successful. His experiment topped six hundred pounds and was so large he could not walk. Poor thing's legs couldn't support his weight. Grandpa got several hands to help drag the beast to the trough so he could eat.

One day, it was decided that the hog should be killed to provide meat for the family, and according to various family members, "That hog sure did eat good." This could be taken at least two different ways.

In my growing-up days, hogs were unjustly ridiculed, vilified, rebuked and made sport of, in everyday phrases such as "He's dirty as a hog," "She's fat as a hog," or "They've gone to the hogs." Hogs were far below the bottom ladder rung of the animal social order, and anybody with the sense of a brass-assed monkey knows they're smarter than horses, dogs and cats.

In recent times I tried to get social and governmental agencies interested in improving the life of the hog, and was near arrested on several occasions. Big-time pigotry was at work here. "Don't bother us with the facts," agency officials said.

Visions of a better place for hogs came to me, and they still do. Upgrade their station in life. Give them something to do. Feed their souls *and* their bellies.

I dreamed of things hogs could be— watchhogs, fine harness hogs, Tennessee Walking hogs, five-gaited hogs, quarter-hogs running between the legs of cows. Lord, the mind reels with possibilities. A hog is much more than the sum of its parts. More than just shoulders, hams, ribs, etc.

Hogs have dreams. Hogs have hopes. And on occasion, hogs are true visionaries.

I believe hogs are filled with poetry, wisdom and romance.

Why, late one afternoon, while walking down a lonely dirt road in rural Tennessee, I heard a soft voice come from just across the fence and it said something like, "Is my body nothing but a shroud for my soul?" And I swear I heard this in plain old English. Not grunts and oinks. Hurrying to see what or who had uttered such a profound statement, I looked over the fence and saw this Duroc deep in thought, apparently pondering the fate of all hogdom. It was then that I knew something very unusual was happening. That very evening the truth about hogs was revealed to me.

This ancient sow told me that humans are spokespersons for hogs, that humans give voice to the thoughts of hogs and that most all authors are in deep trouble once hogs stop communicating with them. Now I'm sure no author is aware of this hog connection, and if he is, he sure isn't going to admit it. Please think about it for just a moment. I'm sure most of you have heard of writer's block. Well, now this explains it. The hogs stop communicating and the writer goes dumber than a turnip.

Although humans get credit for the creation of great prose and poetry, the real credit should go to the hogs. With this in mind, please open your minds to my little offering.

THE QUOTABLE HOG

Stay,

O sweet, and do not rise!
The light that shines
comes from thine eyes.

John Donne

Hog is the name
applied to mammals
of the Suidae fami-
ly. I'm sure you've
heard people yell,
"Sooie, sooie, pig,"
on different occa-
sions. I hope this
clears up where the
hog-calling termi-
nology originated.

Can one desire too much of

a good thing?

Shakespeare

The rankest compound of villainous smell that ever offended nostril.

Shakespeare

No man should be allowed to be pres

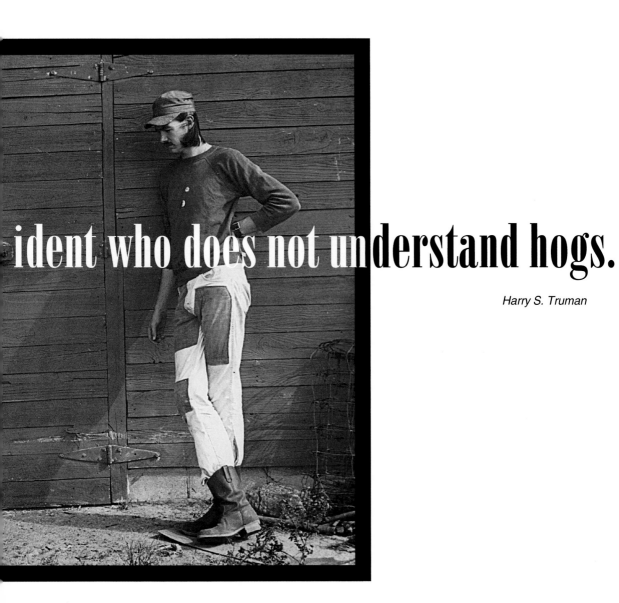

ident who does not understand hogs.

Harry S. Truman

Make me immortal with a kiss!

I

glow fiery bright from the last liaison with my cherub.

Keep my steps steady but dream, dream.

Hark, the he **HOG**, high on the hill. See the she **SOW**, shy and still.

Surging urges, surge and vex.

Hunkering perfection will be no more than now.

Loose the mighty war **HOGS** on this savage land.

Al Clayton

O sleep, O gentle sleep, nature's soft nurse!

Shakespeare

Hogs come in a variety of colors, from black to gray to white, with some red and brown thrown in for variety. Some are solid colors, some spotted, speckled or splotchy. Some, like Hampshires, are belted.

All *hogs* have but one entrance to this world,

and

the same

going out.

Hoggus Maccabee

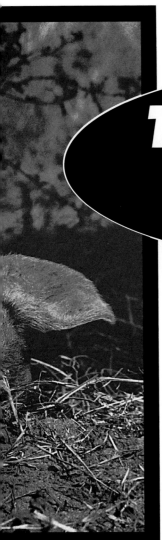

They roll and rumble
They turn and tumble
As piggies do in a poke.

Sir Thomas More

When shall
three meet

we
again?

Shakespeare

She speaks, yet she says

nothing.

He was
most
princely.

Shakespeare

Delicious rooting. Joy without end.
Take my body, America.
Toss my entrails South
(that's where the guts are)
Lob my loins north
(the rich lust after them)
Heave my hams and shoulders east
(the sun will light them first)
Send my snout, ears and tail west.
Great art may flower from my cast-off parts.

Al Clayton

*T*hope to see London once ere I die.

Shakespeare

They are barrel shaped, short legged, coarse bristle coated, short tailed critters with four toes. Bet most of you didn't know the part about the toes. Yep, it's true. Only the middle two have little hooves and are used in walking. They certainly wouldn't be used for sitting or kneeling, would they? Most hogs have about forty-four teeth. The upper and lower canines tend to grow outward and form tusks.

A woman mov'd is like a fountain troubled —

Muddy, ill-seeming, thick, bereft of beauty.

Shakespeare

*B*e near me when my light is low.

Tennyson

Unto you

is

paradise

opened.

The Apocrypha

The gods sent

NOT CORN FOR THE RICH MEN ONLY.

Shakespeare

ROOT, ROOT, ROOT.

The will to root.

The need to root.

The want and right to root.

To drown in rooting.

Endless rooting.

Worlds can be moved

by rooting.

Al Clayton

hat's drinking

mere pause from thinking

And

we are put on earth
a little space
That we may learn to bear
the beams of love.

William Blake

Hogs range from
two to six feet in
length and on occa-
sion achieve a
weight of more than
six hundred pounds.

The lady doth
protest too much,
methinks.

Shakespeare

Journeys end in lovers meeting.

Shakespeare

*L*ove sought is good,
but given unsought, is better.

Shakespeare

Some

great,

are

born

some achieve greatness,

and *some*
have
greatness
thrust
upon them.

Shakespeare

Her lips suck forth my soul.

Christopher Marlowe

Speak of grand days
Long before the fences came.
Before the feed lots and parlors
When the spirit of the great Sow God soared above the
Gulf Stream and the Archangel of Boars was her helpmate.

We were in forests, then, dense and green
with fresh-fallen persimmons and great acorns everywhere.
One had to barely root to find delightful forage.
Meadows with dew-covered spider webs and daffodils
everywhere.
We birthed, slept with, nourished and raised our young
until they chose to find their own way.

Then the people came with a need to control every living
and dead thing.

We are captive from birth to death, heirs of a vile system
that nourishes the lifeblood of the greediest animal of all.
My hooves are unsteady but my sight is clear.
Abandon hope, all who survive birth.

Al Clayton

*T*his was the noblest hog of all.

Al Clayton

Some people say everything on a hog is used except the squeal. We eat the stomach, kidneys, liver, ears, brain, snout, jowls, lips, tongue, throat, lard, intestine, skin, chops, ribs, hams, bacon and shoulders. Tanneries use the skin for leather. The hair is used for brushes, mattresses, air-conditioning filters, baseball gloves. Blood is used to make animal feed, fertilizer and medicine. Drug manufacturers make insulin and other medicine from their glands. The fat is used for everything from shaving cream to lubricating oils, and the bones are ground up for glue and kitty food.

These most brisk and giddy paced times.

Shakespeare

Come home with me to supper.

Shakespeare

Slosh on, ye mig

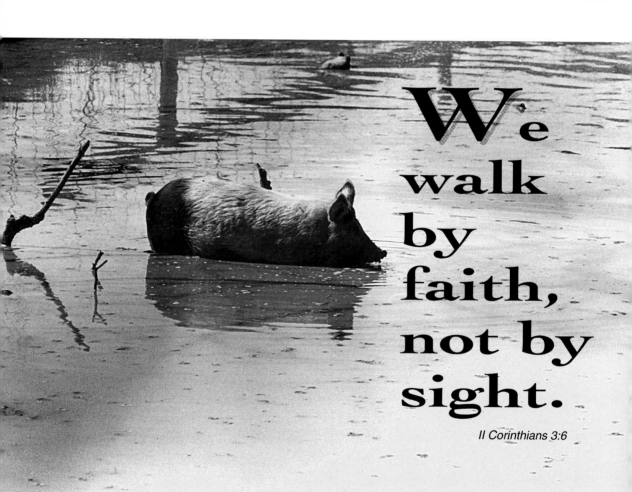

We walk by faith, not by sight.

II Corinthians 3:6

hty ship of state.

Through muck and mire,

through slush and ooze,

my course is true,

not spurred by booze.

Al Clayton

*I*t is ill to drive black hogs in the dark.

Everyman's Dictionary of Quotes and Proverbs

I am the very pink of courtesy.

Shakespeare

It might be a good time for you to become familiar with some hog terms—or to get cheek to jowl, as hogmen are wont to say:

BARROW — a male hog who has been castrated

BOAR — a male hog of any age who has avoided the previous disaster

FARROW — to birth pigs; at this point in time, barrows and boars are incapable of experiencing this joy

GILT — a female hog that has not had a litter and is not over one year old

SHOAT — a young'un that has been weaned from its mother's milk and usually is eight weeks old

My solitude grew more and more obese, like a pig.

Yukio Mishima

Her children rise up and call her

blessed.

Ecclesiastes

Lying sphinx-like, enduring nips from needle teeth. Weariness covers me. The millstone of depression grows heavier by the hour. Responding to Cupid's yowl has left me withered beyond my time. My breasts hang like tired socks.

Al Clayton

What's time to a HOG?

John Egerton

ROOT

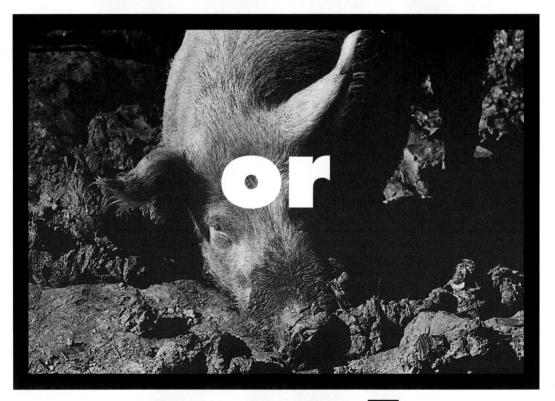

or

DIE!

Tonius Antonius to a group of swineherds

Thoughts on the Death Angel

Most dreadful underwing odor. A stench with great mass and power. A presence so foul, the eyes water and nostrils quiver.

If a feather falls, it poisons the earth it touches.

Al Clayton

Then let thy love be younger than thyself, or thy affection cannot hold the bent.

Shakespeare

About one-fourth of the meat we Americans eat is hog meat, and these hogs eat about one-fifth of the corn that is grown in the United States. Most hogs are raised in corn-producing states like Iowa, Nebraska, Illinois, Indiana, Minnesota, Missouri and Ohio.

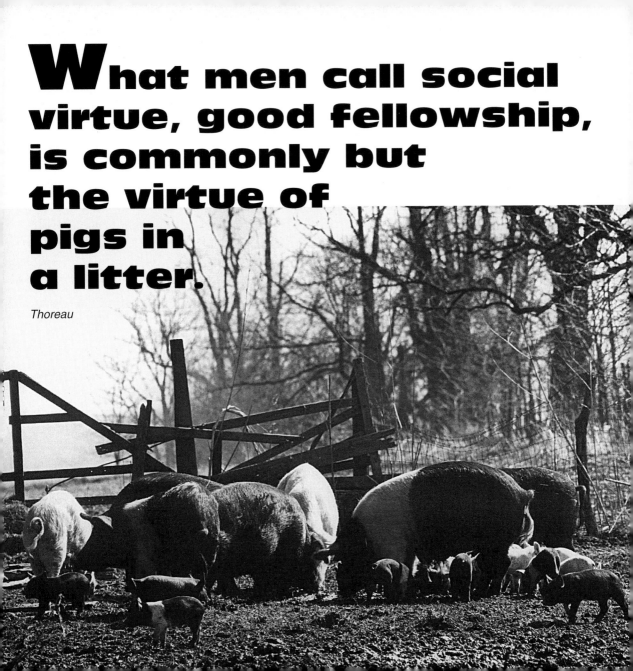

What men call social virtue, good fellowship, is commonly but the virtue of pigs in a litter.

Thoreau

*Great things are done
when hog and earth meet.*

Al Clayton

And so,

from hour to hour, we ripe and ripe, And then from hour to hour we rot and rot; And thereby hangs a tale.

Shakespeare

All the world's a stage.

Shakespeare

As full of spirit as the month of May,

and gorgeous as the sun at midsummer.

Shakespeare

According to a department of the United Nations, there are about 650 million hogs in this world. China has the most, Russia is second, and the United States is third.

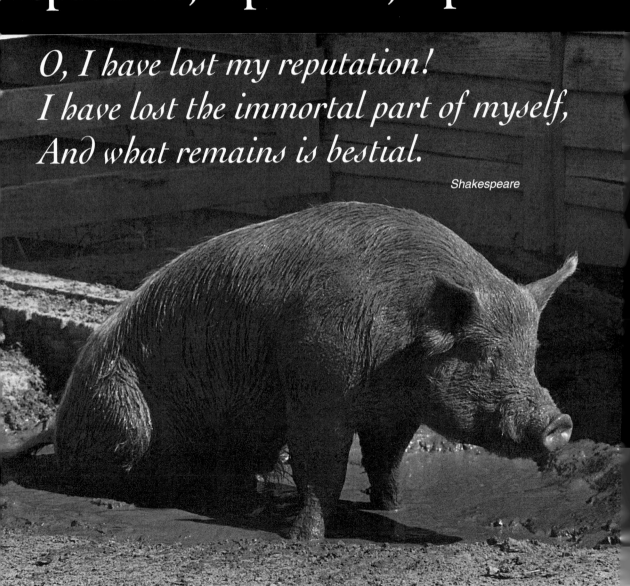

Reputation, reputation, reputation!

O, I have lost my reputation!
I have lost the immortal part of myself,
And what remains is bestial.

Shakespeare

Slop-drenched breezes engulf me.
Flies sense my great hulk and welcome it.

The darkness of my heart hides songs yet to be sung.
Had you sipped from my side of the trough,
the sweet strain of a thousand harps
would have filled the air.
Had you not turned your snout from me
or twitched your tail so indignantly
mute to my needs, confirming my mortality.
I have known you from hock to ear notch.
Once you fell on me like rose petals.
Now we are strangers.

Passionless, clink, clank, creak, clunk, clank, clank.
The sound of death news.
For a morsel to queue up, sustain life so these
nations' heartbeats will continue through the night.

Midnight's clear air intensifies my reality.
Lingering trough smells and cricket chirps.

Al Clayton

Rest, rest, perturbed spirit!

Shakespeare

Is it not strange that desire should so many years outlive performance?

Shakespeare

We

are ne'er like

angels till our

passion dies.

Thomas Dekker

Where the shadow is heavy the whole day through.

Emily Page

There are more than three hundred breeds of pigs; your local library, the Pork Council or the U.S. Department of Agriculture can give you the names.

Whatsoever thy snout findeth to do, do it with thy might.

Song of Solomon

See how he roots, uncovering acorns

strong hammed and handsome,

not shy and retiring.

Thick are his bristles as bamboo in China

His keen sense of smell

makes him a provider.

LEAN
HAMMED
AND OF
TRIM OF
HOCK.

Al Clayton

with better grace,

Shakespeare

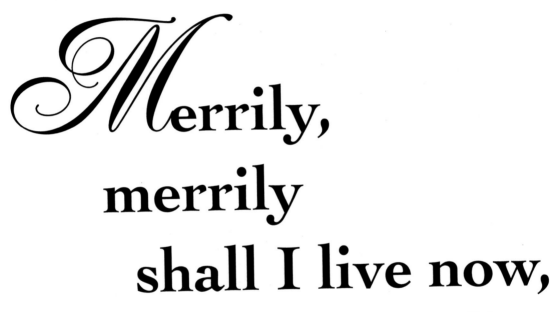

*M*errily, merrily shall I live now,

Shakespeare

under the blossom
that hangs on the bough.

Pigs are said to see the wind. Due to the fact that they have a more acute sense of hearing than humans.

Come live with me, and be my *love.*

Christopher Marlowe

I come with a tail well curled,
with a fine snout and blue eyes.
A worthy warrior, but with a honed sense of beauty.
Hoping to win your grace.
The winter in my heart is exhausted and the sweet season blooms.
You are a violet after an April shower,
My love is an enduring fire, ever burning
In all hogdom, I love you alone.

It is essential that I enter and depart this world alone.
A truly great boar relishes the sweetness of solitude.
Mine is as silent as a falling star.

I am gray and many snows have fallen on my bristles.
Years have not dimmed my vision or shackled my hocks.

Step into blue space and ride the air.
Wind through my bristles electrifies my pork skin.

Such a restless heart. Was earth your home?
Once I was brave and free ranging,
My snout in the wind.
Now my very being is scattered,
Arranged like a spilled purse.
Is my body no more than a shroud for my soul?

He hath eaten me out of house and home.

Shakespeare

A Harvard MBA was waxing one night and made the following observations:
Pig production is based largely on successful breeding. (How else would they get here—maybe in flying saucers?)
The pig is the most economical converter of feed into pork. (Well, it sure ain't gonna turn corn into okra.)

Accept the place the divine providence has found for you.

Emerson

Let us not burden our remembrances with a **heaviness** that's gone.

Shakespeare

Neither life nor death

can harm a great hog.

Swinus McFee

*S*he sat like patience on a monument, smiling at grief.

Shakespeare

Sorrow owns the last hours.

Gaze at a bleak sky and
wait the end that's sure.
Could I seek to slumber or
gaze at countless stars,
Sentenced to this parched scape,
heir to a quenchless maw.
The earth is dear to us and
we are its gift.

Al Clayton

Nature teaches

beasts to know
their friends.

Shakespeare

Al Clayton is the photographer of the best-selling gourmet spoofs *Critter Cuisine* and *Dreadful Delicacies*. He is also one of America's most respected photographers; his work has appeared in *Look*, *Time*, *Newsweek*, and *Life* magazines. He was awarded the Overseas Press Club Citation for Excellence for his coverage of the war in Biafra for *Look*.

Raised among fine hogs in rural Tennessee, Clayton's affection for the fair and bristled creature runs deep. The plight of his porcine pals has long eaten at Al, and with this book he fulfills his desire to make their voices heard.